Artificial intelligence (AI)

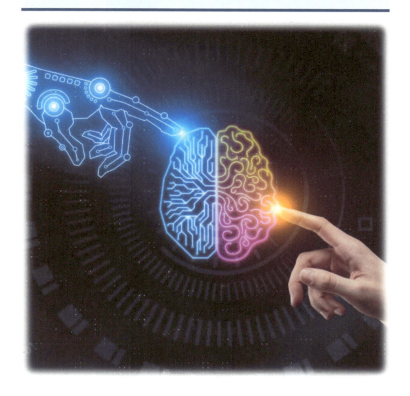

KNOWLEDGE

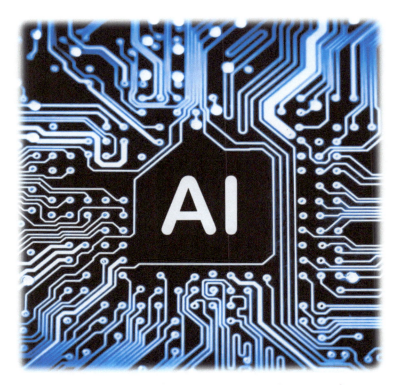

"AI will be the most transformative technology of the 21st century. It will affect every industry and aspect of our lives."

Jensen Huang, co-founder & CEO of NVIDIA

Disclaimer

Please be informed that every effort has been made to ensure the accuracy and completeness of the information presented in this text. However, error is inevitable, and we apologize in advance for any typographical errors or factual inaccuracies that may have inadvertently slipped through. We kindly request that readers bring any such errors to our attention, and we will promptly correct them.

Similarly, when applicable, we have strived to properly attribute all textual and visual content. If any credits have been omitted or misattributed, please inform us so that we may rectify the oversight.

It is important to note that this collection does not purport to be an exhaustive exploration of the subject matter. To delve deeper into specific topics and explore additional resources, we encourage readers to consult the references and further reading suggestions provided.

Foreword

Welcome to this new volume of **the essentials-Knowledge**, a series dedicated to providing clear, concise, and accurate insights into the most pressing issues of our time.

Our goal is to provide a concise overview of the current state-of-the-art and to make complex topics accessible to a wide audience, fostering a deeper understanding of the world around us.

the essentials, our new collection, is designed and directed by **Renaud Neurtolz**. Author, editor and technical translator for almost 15 years, Renaud is literally, as his brother-in-law puts it, a "Renaissance man". To date, his writings on a variety of subjects have been sold in 8 countries (Belgium, Canada, France, Germany, Luxembourg, Netherlands, Spain, Switzerland and the USA).

Curious about everything, passionate about general culture and human creativity in all its forms, as well as the wonders of nature, Renaud is the ideal candidate to manage and develop this collection, whose spirit suits him perfectly. When his "French touch" meets the world and brings it to you through **the essentials**, we can only hope for the best!

the essentials collection is made up of several categories (**the essentials-Essay, the essentials-Knowledge, the essentials-People and the essentials-Q&A**) to bring everyone the style of reading they like best.

In addition, recognizing that people learn in different ways, we produce, by ourselves or in collaboration, **videos** and **podcasts** (on our YouTube channel @thessentialscollection), offering alternative perspectives and additional information on the various topics we cover.

The **podcast** and **video** will not be identical to the **eBook** and **printed book** (on Amazon) version but will be variations of the same subject that will help provide different viewpoints and better memorize the theme thanks to the stimulation of several of our senses (by reading, listening and watching). Moreover, we plan to have them translated into several major languages in the future...

This collection is a testament to our commitment to knowledge dissemination. We believe that everyone, regardless of their background, deserves access to information that is both accurate, informative, and engaging. Through this series, we hope to spark curiosity, inspire critical thinking, and empower individuals to make informed decisions.

As you delve into the different volumes of this collection, you will encounter a diverse range of subjects, from the latest advancements in technology to the timeless wisdom of philosophical thought. Each piece has been carefully crafted to provide a balanced perspective, drawing on the expertise of leading thinkers and researchers.

We invite you to embark on this intellectual and emotional journey with us. May you find the insights within these pages as enlightening as we did when designing them.

We deeply thank you for your trust, time, support, and feedback! the essentials

A word from the editor...

It leaves no one indifferent! Everyone talks about it! Everyone wants to understand it! Everyone has questions and strong opinions on the subject! Artificial intelligence (AI) raises fears and hopes that go beyond what is considered logical or reasonable! It has already changed our lives in many ways, some of which are beyond our understanding and knowledge. It will continue to reshape and revolutionize every aspect of our lives at an even faster pace in the years to come. Beyond the myths, let us explore what AI really is, its promises and its dangers in the light of current knowledge. It could be different sooner than we think...

Please, feel free to consult the various resources on this subject (eBook, printed book, video and podcast), which will provide you with a range of interesting perspectives.

Thank you for your confidence and enthusiasm!

Table of contents

Illustration credits & references

A special thanks for the following online resources that have helped shape the visual world of this document and make its contents so much better!

- ✓ https://www.canva.com
  (Canva Pro version: for some original & altered illustrations)

- ✓ https://notebooklm.google.com
  (Public version: for our "mini podcasts")

- ✓ https://ai.invideo.io
  (Invideo AI Plus: for our short videos)

- ✓ https://gemini.google.com
  (Public version: for some content creation)

- ✓ https://chat.mistral.ai/chat
  (public version: for some content creation)

- ✓ https://chatgpt.com/gpts
  (Public version: for some content creation)

- ✓ https://claude.ai
  (Public version: for some content creation)

Specifically for this printed book, eBook and PDF:

- ✓ https://www.researchgate.net
- ✓ https://deltalogix.blog/en
- ✓ https://seattlewebsitedesign.medium.com
- ✓ https://towardsdatascience.com
- ✓ https://medium.com
- ✓ https://www.linkedin.com
- ✓ https://www.euriun.com
- ✓ https://www.orangemantra.com
- ✓ https://www.statista.com
- ✓ https://www.geo.fr
- ✓ https://fr.wikipedia.org
- ✓ https://www.ibm.com
- ✓ https://aws.amazon.com
- ✓ https://peak.ai
- ✓ https://autogpt.net
- ✓ https://www.forbes.com

Document information

- ✓ Title: "**Artificial intelligence (AI)**" – V1.1 – the essentials-Knowledge – Renaud Neurtolz – December 16, 2024.
- ✓ ISBN: 9798304237079.

"As artificial intelligence evolves, we must remember that its power lies not in replacing human intelligence, but in augmenting it. The true potential of AI lies in its ability to amplify human creativity and ingenuity."

Ginni Rometty, executive chairman of IBM

Primer

What is artificial intelligence (AI)?

Artificial intelligence is a branch of computer science dedicated to creating intelligent agents, systems that can reason, learn, and act autonomously. In essence, AI aims to simulate human intelligence in machines.

Key concepts in AI

- ✓ **Machine learning (ML):** A subset of AI that enables systems to learn from data without explicit programming.

  - ○ **Supervised learning (SL):** Trains models on labeled data to make predictions.

  - ○ **Unsupervised learning (UL):** Discovers patterns in unlabeled data.

  - ○ **Reinforcement learning (RL):** Agents learn through trial and error, receiving rewards or penalties.

- ✓ **Deep learning (DL):** A subset of machine learning that uses artificial neural networks with multiple layers to process complex data.

- ✓ **Natural language processing (NLP):** Enables machines to understand, interpret, and generate human language.

- ✓ **Computer vision:** Allows machines to interpret and understand visual information from the world.

- ✓ **Large language models (LLMs):** A category of foundation models (a subset of deep learning and generative AI) trained on very large amounts of data making them capable of understanding and generating natural language and various types of content to perform a wide range of tasks.

A brief history of AI

The concept of AI dates back to ancient civilizations, but its modern form emerged in the mid-20th century. Key milestones include:

- ✓ **1956:** The Dartmouth Conference, where the term "artificial intelligence" was coined.

- ✓ **1960s-1970s:** Early AI research focused on symbolic AI, attempting to represent knowledge and reason using logical rules.

- ✓ **1980s-1990s:** The rise of expert systems, AI programs designed to solve complex problems within a specific domain.

✓ **2000s-Present:** The resurgence of AI, driven by advancements in machine learning, deep learning, and big data.

Key players and forms of AI

✓ **Tech giants:** Companies like Google, Microsoft, Amazon, NVIDIA, IBM, and Meta are heavily investing in AI research and development.

✓ **Startups:** Numerous startups are focused on specific AI applications, from healthcare to finance.

✓ **Research institutions:** Universities and research labs worldwide contribute to AI advancements.

AI tools and applications

✓ **AI Tools:**

  ○ **TensorFlow or PyTorch, etc. :** Popular frameworks for building and training machine learning models...

  ○ **OpenAI's GPT-4, LLaMA 3 or Mixtral 8x7b, etc. :** Powerful language models capable of generating human-quality text...

  ○ **DALL-E 3 or Flux 1, etc. :** AI systems that generate images from text descriptions...

✓ **AI Applications:**

- ○ **Healthcare:** Disease diagnosis, drug discovery, personalized medicine.

- ○ **Finance:** Fraud detection, algorithmic trading, risk assessment.

- ○ **Autonomous vehicles:** Self-driving cars and trucks.

- ○ **Customer service:** Chatbots and virtual assistants.

- ○ **Entertainment:** Game development, content creation, recommendation systems.

The future of AI: Challenges and risks

While AI holds immense potential, it also presents challenges and risks:

- ✓ **Ethical concerns:** Bias in AI algorithms, job displacement, and the misuse of AI for malicious purposes.

- ✓ **Technical limitations:** AI systems can be vulnerable to adversarial attacks and require significant computational resources.

- ✓ **Regulatory challenges:** Developing appropriate regulations to govern AI development and deployment.

Conclusion

Artificial intelligence is rapidly transforming our world, offering unprecedented opportunities and complex challenges. As AI continues to evolve, it is crucial to harness its power responsibly and ethically to benefit society as a whole.

"Artificial intelligence, deep learning, machine learning — whatever you're doing if you don't understand it — learn it. Because otherwise, you're going to be a dinosaur within three years."

Mark Cuban, American entrepreneur & investor

Module 1: Foundations of AI

1.1 What is AI?

1.1.1 A brief history of AI

- ✓ **Early AI:** The birth of AI in the 1950s and 1960s, focusing on symbolic AI and rule-based systems.

- ✓ **"AI winter":** Periods of reduced funding and interest in AI research.

- ✓ **"AI spring":** The resurgence of AI in the 1980s and 1990s, driven by advances in machine learning.

- ✓ **The AI boom:** The current era of AI, characterized by breakthroughs in deep learning and its widespread applications.

1.1.2 Defining AI

- ✓ **Definition:** Artificial intelligence is a set of theories and techniques aimed at creating machines capable of simulating human intelligence. It is the use of computer systems or machines that have some of the qualities that the human brain has, such as the ability to interpret and produce language in a way that seems human, recognize or create images, sounds, and videos, solve various problems, learn from data supplied to them, etc.

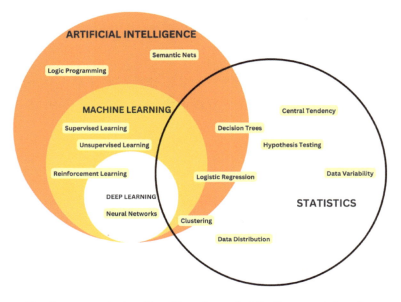

Venn diagram depicting the conceptual overlap between AI, machine learning (ML), deep learning (DL), and statistics, with examples of algorithms within each category. Broadly, AI encompasses algorithms that aim to mimic human decision-making, with ML being a subset that learns patterns from data without explicit instructions. DL refers to neural-network-based algorithms. AI and statistics share a base in probability theory.

✓ **Narrow AI (weak AI):** AI systems designed to perform specific tasks.

- ✓ **General AI (strong AI):** AI systems with human-level intelligence and the ability to understand and learn any intellectual task.

- ✓ **Superintelligence:** AI systems that surpass human intelligence in every aspect.

Three types of Artificial Intelligence

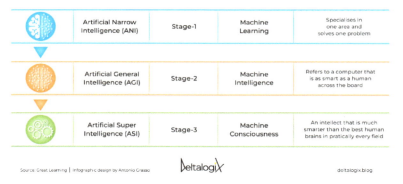

	Artificial Narrow Intelligence (ANI)	Stage-1	Machine Learning	Specialises in one area and solves one problem
	Artificial General Intelligence (AGI)	Stage-2	Machine Intelligence	Refers to a computer that is as smart as a human across the board
	Artificial Super Intelligence (ASI)	Stage-3	Machine Consciousness	An intellect that is much smarter than the best human brains in pratically every field

Source: Great Learning | Infographic design by Antonio Grasso   Deltalogix   deltalogix.blog

https://deltalogix.blog/en/2023/03/08/artificial-intelligence-a-look-at-its-three-types-and-their-possible-future-implications/

The three proposed types of AI.

1.1.3 The Turing test

- ✓ A test of a machine's ability to exhibit intelligent behavior equivalent to, or indistinguishable from, that of a human.

- ✓ **Limitations of the Turing test:** It focuses on linguistic ability and does not assess reasoning, problem-solving, or creativity.

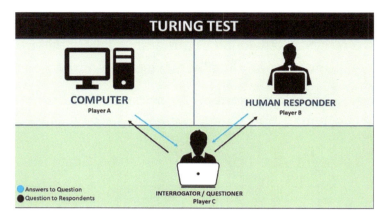

How does the Turing test work?

✓ Alan Mathison Turing (1912-1954) was a British mathematician and cryptologist, author of works that scientifically founded computer science. Among his many achievements, he helped foil the plans of the Germans during the Second World War, by deciphering the encrypted messages of their famous "Enigma" cryptographic machine. He is also a pioneer of artificial intelligence.

1.2 Key concepts in AI

The artificial intelligence (AI) lifecycle has 3 primary phases: to design, to develop, and to deploy. These phases are further partitioned into a series of stages, beginning with data collection and selection; data annotation; and proceeding through machine learning (ML) model design and creation, testing and evaluation, deployment and operationalization, and monitoring and integration of feedback loops for continuous improvement. Human-centered AI can help recognize and remediate the sources of bias that induce health disparities and inequities that can arise at each stage.

1.2.1 Machine learning (ML)

✓ **Supervised learning (SL):** Training models on labeled data to make predictions or decisions.

- o **Regression:** Predicting a continuous numerical value.

- o **Classification:** Categorizing data into discrete classes.

✓ **Unsupervised learning (UL):** Discovering patterns in unlabeled data.

- o **Clustering:** Grouping similar data points together.

- o **Dimensionality reduction:** Reducing the number of features in data.

✓ **Reinforcement learning (RL):** Learning through trial and error, receiving rewards or penalties for actions.

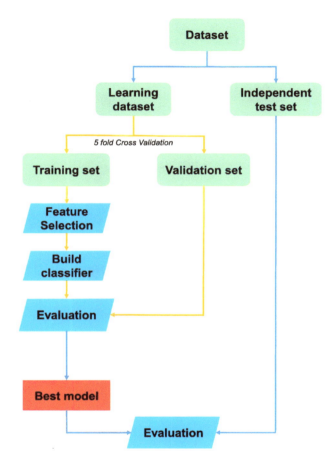

Flowchart of the machine learning (ML) process used to assess the performance of each algorithm tested. Each dataset is initially split into two subsets: the "Learning dataset" and the "Independent test set". Subsequently, the former undergoes a 5-fold cross validation strategy, where "Training" sets are used to select informative features ("Feature selection") and "Validation" sets to test the classifier performance ("Evaluation"). Finally, the "Best model" is

selected and then, assessed on the "Independent test set" ("Evaluation"): the last evaluation step is used to compare the performance of each feature selection method.

1.2.2 Deep learning (DL)

- ✓ **Neural networks (NNs):** Inspired by the human brain, neural networks are composed of interconnected nodes called neurons.

- ✓ **Convolutional neural networks (CNNs):** Specialized for image and video recognition tasks.

- ✓ **Recurrent neural networks (RNNs):** Designed to process sequential data, such as text and time series.

- ✓ **Generative adversarial networks (GANs):** A framework for training generative models, often used for image and video generation.

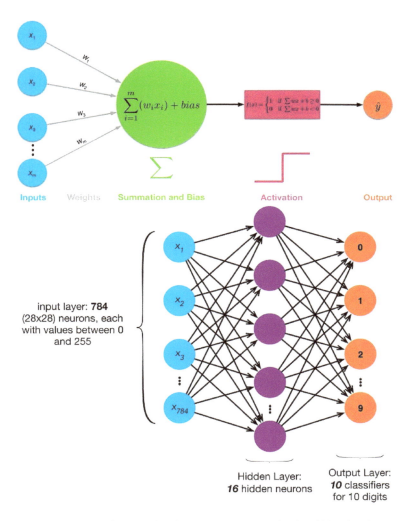

input layer: **784** (28x28) neurons, each with values between 0 and 255

Inputs   Weights   Summation and Bias   Activation   Output

Hidden Layer: **16** hidden neurons

Output Layer: **10** classifiers for 10 digits

https://towardsdatascience.com/multi-layer-neural-networks-with-sigmoid-function-deep-learning-for-rookies-2-bf464f09eb7f

Multi-layer neural networks with sigmoid function - deep learning for rookies.

1.2.3 Natural language processing (NLP)

- ✓ **Text classification:** Categorizing text documents (e.g., sentiment analysis, spam detection).

- ✓ **Machine translation:** Translating text from one language to another.

- ✓ **Text generation:** Generating human-quality text, such as articles or poetry.

- ✓ **Speech recognition:** Converting spoken language into text.

- ✓ **Text-to-speech:** Synthesizing speech from text.

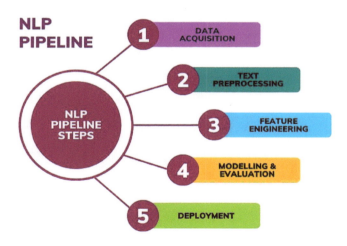

Understanding the NLP pipeline.

1.2.4 Computer vision

- ✓ **Image classification:** Identifying objects and scenes in images.

- ✓ **Object detection:** Locating and identifying objects within images.

- ✓ **Image segmentation:** Dividing an image into meaningful regions.

- ✓ **Image generation:** Creating new images from scratch or modifying existing ones.

1.2.5 Large language models (LLMs)

- ✓ **Large language models (LLMs):** Are powerful learning models (a subset of deep learning and generative AI) that are pre-trained on vast amounts of data from sources like Common Crawl and Wikipedia (hundreds of billions of pages).
- ✓ **With billions of parameters:** LLMs are based on transformer neural networks that can extract meaning and understand relationships within text sequences. These LLM transformers can be trained in an unsupervised manner, enabling them to learn grammar, language, and background knowledge.
- ✓ **Thanks to their parallel processing capabilities:** LLMs can be trained using GPUs, significantly reducing the training time.

✓ **LLMs have a wide range of applications:** Including generative AI that can produce content based on human language instructions.

✓ **They are incredibly versatile:** They can perform tasks like answering questions, summarizing documents, and translating languages. LLMs are transforming various areas such as content creation, search engine usage, and virtual assistants.

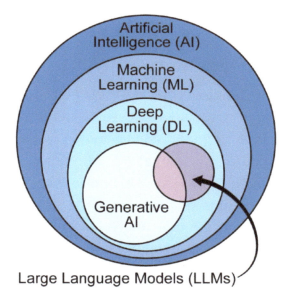

LLMs within the AI taxonomy...

1.3 AI algorithms and techniques

1.3.1 Search algorithms

- ✓ **Uninformed search:**

  - o **Breadth-first search (BFS):** Explores all nodes at a given depth before moving to the next depth.

  - o **Depth-first search (DFS):** Explores as deep as possible along a branch before backtracking.

- ✓ **Informed search:**

  - o **A* (informed search algorithm):** Uses a heuristic function to guide the search towards the goal.

  - o **Greedy best-first search:** Selects the node with the lowest estimated cost to the goal.

1.3.2 Optimization algorithms

- ✓ **Gradient descent (GD):** An iterative optimization algorithm used to find the minimum of a function.

  - o **Stochastic gradient descent (SGD):** A variant of gradient descent that updates parameters using a single data point at a time.

○ **Mini-batch gradient descent (MBGD):** A compromise between batch and stochastic gradient descent, using small batches of data.

1.3.3 Bayesian inference

- ✓ A statistical method for inferring probabilities of events based on prior knowledge and new evidence.

- ✓ **Bayesian networks:** Graphical models that represent probabilistic relationships between variables.

1.3.4 Decision trees and random forests

- ✓ **Decision trees:** Tree-like models of decisions and their possible consequences.

- ✓ **Random forests:** An ensemble method that combines multiple decision trees to improve accuracy and reduce overfitting.

1.3.5 Support vector machines (SVMs)

- ✓ A supervised learning algorithm used for classification and regression tasks.

- ✓ SVMs find the optimal hyperplane that separates data points into different classes.

"By understanding these core algorithms and techniques, you can build and implement effective AI systems."

Example of AI-generated image...

"This next generation of AI will reshape every software category and every business, including our own. Although this new era promises great opportunity, it demands even greater responsibility from companies like ours."

Satya Nadella, CEO of Microsoft

Module 2: AI in action: real-world applications

https://www.linkedin.com/pulse/ai-tools-action-real-world-applications-success-post-mukherjee-u1f4c/

AI tools in action: Real-world applications.

2.1 AI in healthcare

- ✓ **Medical diagnosis:** AI-powered systems can analyze medical images (X-rays, CT scans, MRIs) to detect diseases like cancer, heart disease, and neurological disorders.

- ✓ **Drug discovery:** AI algorithms can accelerate drug discovery by analyzing vast amounts of biological data to identify potential drug candidates.

✓ **Personalized medicine:** AI can analyze patient data to tailor treatments to individual needs, improving outcomes and reducing side effects.

✓ **Healthcare robotics:** AI-powered robots can assist in surgeries, rehabilitation, and patient care.

2.2 AI in finance

✓ **Algorithmic trading:** AI algorithms can analyze market data and execute trades at high speed, often outperforming human traders.

✓ **Fraud detection:** AI can identify patterns in financial transactions to detect fraudulent activity.

✓ **Risk assessment:** AI models can assess credit risk, insurance risk, and other financial risks.

✓ **Chatbots for customer service:** AI-powered chatbots can provide 24/7 customer support and answer queries.

2.3 AI in autonomous vehicles

✓ **Sensor fusion:** Combining data from various sensors (camera, LiDAR, RADAR) to create a comprehensive understanding of the environment.

✓ **Computer vision:** Identifying objects, traffic signs, pedestrians and animals using image and video processing techniques.

✓ **Motion planning and control:** Planning safe and efficient driving maneuvers.

2.4 AI in natural language processing (NLP)

✓ **Machine translation:** Translating text from one language to another.

✓ **Sentiment analysis:** Determining the sentiment (positive, negative, neutral) of texts.

✓ **Text summarization:** Condensing long texts into shorter summaries.

✓ **Chatbots and virtual assistants:** Interacting with users in natural language.

2.5 AI in computer vision

✓ **Image and video recognition:** Identifying objects and scenes in images and videos.

✓ **Object detection:** Locating and identifying objects within images and videos.

✓ **Facial recognition:** Identifying individuals based on their facial features.

✓ **Image generation:** Creating new images or modifying existing ones.

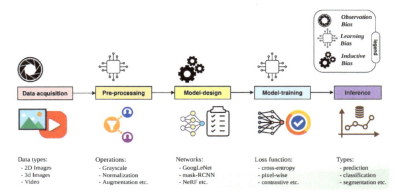

Computer vision pipeline showing different biases and different points of physics incorporation in PICV applications.

"By understanding these real-world applications, you can appreciate the transformative power of AI and its potential to shape the future."

Example of AI-generated image...

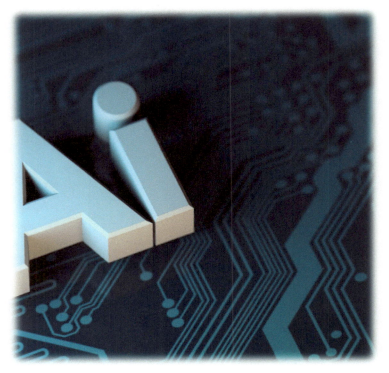

"We must address, individually and collectively, moral and ethical issues raised by cutting-edge research in artificial intelligence and biotechnology... which will enable significant life extension, designer babies, and memory extraction."

Klaus Martin Schwab, founder of the World Economic Forum

Module 3: Ethical considerations & societal impact

| Fairness | Reliability | Transparency | Privacy | Inclusivity | Accountable | Oversight | Environmental Well-being |

https://www.euriun.com/ai-guidelines/

Ethical guidelines for trustworthy artificial intelligence (AI).

3.1 Bias and fairness in AI

- ✓ **Algorithmic bias:** AI systems can perpetuate biases present in training data, leading to unfair and discriminatory outcomes.

- ✓ **Fairness metrics:** Developing metrics to measure fairness and mitigate bias in AI systems.

- ✓ **Mitigating bias in AI systems:** Techniques like data augmentation, fairness constraints, and algorithmic fairness.

3.2 Job displacement and economic impact

- ✓ **The impact of AI on the job market:** AI automation can lead to job displacement in certain industries.

✓ **Reskilling and upskilling:** The need for workers to acquire new skills to adapt to the changing job market.

✓ **The potential for AI to create new jobs:** AI can create new industries and job opportunities.

3.3 AI safety and security

✓ **Adversarial attacks:** Malicious attacks aimed at manipulating AI systems.

✓ **AI safety guidelines:** Developing guidelines for safe and responsible AI development.

✓ **Responsible AI development:** Prioritizing safety and security in AI research and deployment.

3.4 AI and privacy

✓ **Data privacy and security:** Protecting sensitive data used to train and operate AI systems.

✓ **Ethical use of AI in surveillance:** Balancing the benefits of surveillance with privacy concerns.

"By understanding the ethical considerations and societal impact of AI, we can direct it for a future where AI will not be detrimental to our lives."

Example of AI-generated image...

"Artificial intelligence holds immense promise for tackling some of society's most pressing challenges, from climate change to healthcare disparities. Let's leverage AI responsibly to create a more equitable world."

Katherine Gorman, co-founder & producer of 'Talking Machines'

Module 4: AI & society

How AI is changing our society.

4.1 AI and the workforce

- ✓ **Job displacement and creation:** Analyzing the potential impact of AI on various industries.

- ✓ **Skill gap and reskilling:** Identifying the skills needed for the AI era and strategies for reskilling workers.

- ✓ **The future of work:** Exploring new work models and the role of AI in the future of work.

4.2 AI and education

- ✓ **Personalized learning:** Using AI to tailor education to individual student needs.

- ✓ **Intelligent tutoring systems:** Developing AI-powered tutoring systems.

- ✓ **AI-assisted education:** Leveraging AI to enhance teaching and learning.

4.3 AI and creativity

- ✓ **AI-generated art and music:** Exploring the creative potential of AI.

- ✓ **AI as a tool for human creativity:** Using AI to augment human creativity.

- ✓ **Ethical considerations in AI-generated creativity:** Addressing issues of copyright, originality, and intellectual property.

4.4 AI and global challenges

- ✓ **Sustainable development and climate change:** Using AI to develop solutions to these crucial questions.

- ✓ **Healthcare:** Applying AI to improve healthcare access and outcomes.

✓ **Poverty and inequality:** Leveraging AI to reduce poverty and inequality.

✓ **Eco-friendliness:** Mitigating the energy and resource consumption of AI systems themselves.

"By understanding the societal implications of AI, we can work towards a future where AI benefits humanity as a whole."

"Success in creating effective AI could be the biggest event in the history of our civilization. Or the worst. We just don't know."

Stephen Hawking, theoretical physicist, cosmologist & author

Module 5: The future of AI

Preparing for the future of AI.

5.1 Emerging trends

- ✓ **Explainable AI:** Developing AI models that can explain their decision-making process.

- ✓ **Reinforcement learning from human feedback (RLHF):** Training AI models through human feedback to improve their behavior.

- ✓ **Neuro-symbolic AI:** Combining the strengths of neural networks and symbolic AI to create more intelligent systems.

- ✓ **Quantum AI:** Leveraging quantum computing to accelerate AI research and development.

5.2 Challenges and opportunities

✓ **The need for more data and computational power:** To train large and complex AI models.

✓ **Ethical considerations and regulatory challenges:** Addressing the ethical implications of AI and developing appropriate regulations.

✓ **The potential for AI to solve global problems:** AI can be used to address climate change, sustainable development, healthcare, and other global challenges.

5.3 Preparing for the AI future

✓ **Lifelong learning and adaptability:** The importance of continuous learning and adapting to the changing landscape of AI.

✓ **Ethical AI development and deployment:** Prioritizing ethical considerations in AI research and development.

✓ **Collaboration between humans and AI:** Fostering effective collaboration between humans and AI systems.

The Future Of A.I.

Forecasted cumulative global artificial intelligence revenue 2016-2025, by use case (U.S. dollars)

Use case	Revenue
Static image recognition, classification, and tagging	$8,097.9m
Algorithmic trading strategy performance improvement	$7,540.5m
Efficient, scalable processing of patient data	$7,366.4m
Predictive maintenance	$4,680.3m
Object identification, detection, classification, tracking'	$4,201.0m
Text query of images	$3,714.1m
Automated geophysical feature detection	$3,655.5m
Content distribution on social media	$3,566.6m
Object detection and classification - avoidance, navigation	$3,169.8m
Prevention against cybersecurity threats	$2,472.6m

* From geospatial images
@StatistaCharts   Source: Tractica

statista

https://www.statista.com/chart/6810/the-future-of-ai/

The future of AI.

"By understanding the emerging trends and challenges in AI, we can prepare for a future where AI plays an increasingly important role in our lives."

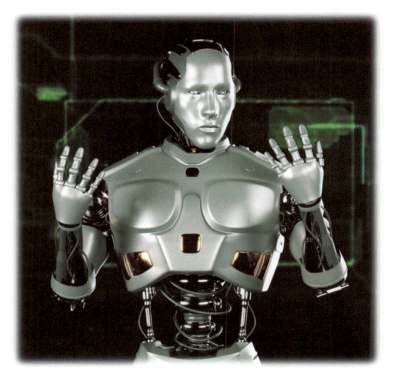

"Responsible AI is not just about liability — it's about ensuring what you are building is enabling human flourishing."

Rumman Chowdhury, CEO of Parity AI

Resources

✓ **Books/eBooks:**

- ○ **"Artificial Intelligence: A Modern Approach"** by Stuart Russell and Peter Norvig

- ○ **"Deep Learning"** by Ian Goodfellow, Yoshua Bengio, and Aaron Courville

- ○ **"The Master Algorithm"** by Pedro Domingos

✓ **Online courses:**

- ○ **Coursera**

- ○ **edX**

- ○ **Udacity**

- ○ **Google AI**

✓ **YouTube channels:**

- ○ **3Blue1Brown**

- ○ **Sentdex**

- ○ **Machine Learning Mastery**

"Artificial intelligence is not just about efficiency gains, it's about opening up new possibilities, unlocking human potential and solving some of society's biggest challenges."

Yoshua Bengio, computer scientist & Turing Award laureate

Glossary

A

- ✓ **Artificial intelligence (AI):** The science and engineering of making intelligent machines, especially intelligent computer programs.

- ✓ **Algorithm:** A step-by-step procedure for solving a problem or accomplishing a task.

- ✓ **Artificial neural network (ANN):** A computational model inspired by the structure and function of the human brain.

- ✓ **Augmented intelligence:** The enhancement of human cognitive abilities through AI technologies.

B

- ✓ **Backpropagation:** An algorithm used to train artificial neural networks.

- ✓ **Bayesian inference:** A statistical method for inferring probabilities of events based on prior knowledge and new evidence.

- ✓ **Bias:** A machine learning model's tendency to favor certain outcomes over others.

C

✓ **Computer vision:** The field of AI that enables computers to interpret and understand visual information from the world.

✓ **Convolutional neural network (CNN):** A type of neural network used for image and video recognition.

✓ **Clustering:** The task of grouping a set of objects in such a way that objects in the same group (cluster) are more similar (in some sense or another) to each other than to those in other groups.

D

✓ **Data mining:** The process of discovering patterns in large data sets involving methods at the intersection of machine learning, statistics, and database systems.

✓ **Deep learning (DL):** A subset of machine learning that uses artificial neural networks with multiple layers to learn complex patterns from data.

✓ **Decision tree:** A tree-like model of decisions and their possible consequences.

F

✓ **Feature engineering:** The process of selecting and transforming features to improve model performance.

✓ **Feature extraction:** The process of automatically selecting the most relevant features from a dataset.

G

✓ **Gradient descent:** An optimization algorithm used to minimize a function.

✓ **Generative adversarial network (GAN):** A class of machine learning frameworks designed by Ian Goodfellow and his colleagues in 2014.

L

✓ **Large language models (LLMs):** A category of foundation models (a subset of deep learning and generative AI) trained on immense amounts of data making them capable of understanding and generating natural language and other types of content to perform a wide range of tasks.

M

- ✓ **Machine learning (ML):** A field of computer science that gives computers the ability to learn without being explicitly programmed.

- ✓ **Model:** A mathematical representation of a real-world system.

N

- ✓ **Natural language processing (NLP):** A field of computer science and artificial intelligence concerned with the interactions between computers and human (natural) languages.

- ✓ **Neural network (NN):** A network of interconnected units called neurons.

O

- ✓ **Overfitting:** A phenomenon that occurs when a model is too complex and fits the training data too closely, leading to poor performance on new data.

R

- ✓ **Reinforcement learning (RL):** A machine learning method where an agent learns to make decisions by interacting with an environment through trial and error, receiving rewards or penalties.

✓ **Recurrent neural network (RNN):** A type of neural network designed to process sequential data.

S

✓ **Supervised learning (SL):** A type of machine learning where a model is trained on labeled data.

✓ **Support vector machine (SVM):** A supervised machine learning model that analyzes data used for classification and regression analysis.

U

✓ **Unsupervised learning (UL):** A type of machine learning where a model is trained on unlabeled data.

V

✓ **Validation set:** A subset of data used to evaluate the performance of a model during training.

Example of AI-generated image...

To keep the story going...

I thought it would be useful to give here two of the most striking quotes on AI, one quite pessimistic and the other very optimistic!

"The development of full artificial intelligence could spell the end of the human race. It would take off on its own, and re-design itself at an ever-increasing rate. Humans, who are limited by slow biological evolution, couldn't compete, and would be superseded."

Stephen Hawking, theoretical physicist, cosmologist & author

"Generative AI has the potential to change the world in ways that we can't even imagine. It has the power to create new ideas, products, and services that will make our lives easier, more productive, and more creative. It also has the potential to solve some of the world's biggest problems, such as climate change, poverty, and disease."

Bill Gates, businessman, philanthropist & co-founder of Microsoft

Example of AI-generated image...

We hope you enjoyed this reading...
Stay tuned for our next exciting topic!!

www.ingramcontent.com/pod-product-compliance
Lightning Source LLC
LaVergne TN
LVHW072050060326

832903LV00053B/314